IMMIGRATION TODAY

WHY DO PEOPLE MOVE TO THE UK?

Nancy Dickmann

raintree

a Capstone company — publishers for children

Raintree is an imprint of Capstone Global Library Limited, a company incorporated in England and Wales having its registered office at 264 Banbury Road, Oxford, OX2 7DY – Registered company number: 6695582

myorders@raintree.co.uk

Text © Capstone Global Library Limited 2019
The moral rights of the proprietor have been asserted

Edited by Clare Lewis
Designed by Dynamo Limited
Original illustrations © Capstone Global Library Limited 2019
Picture research by Dynamo Limited
Production by Kathy McColley
Originated by Capstone Global Library Limited
Printed and bound in India

ISBN 978 1 4747 7299 0 (hardcover)
ISBN 978 1 4747 7300 3 (paperback)

British Library Cataloguing in Publication Data
A full catalogue record for this book is available from the British Library

Acknowledgements
We would like to thank the following for permission to reproduce photographs:
Alamy: Alex Segre, 22, Bob Daemmrich Photography/Marjorie Kamys Cotera, 18, Graham Jepson, 23, Robert Oates, 19; Getty Images: AFP/Delil Souleiman, 9, AFP/Jack Guez, 13, AFP/Tolga Akmen, 25, Barcroft Media/Geovien So, 15, Charles McQuillan, 28, Daily Herald Archive/SSPL, 8, E+/sturti, 10, E+/tolgart, 27, iStock, 1, iStock/AdrianHancu, 16, iStock/DaLiu, 7, iStock/designer491, 26, iStock/Drimafilm, 21, iStock/Gannet77, 6, iStock/lovemax, 29, iStock/Steve Debenport, 5, Leon Neal, 24, NurPhoto/Nicolas Economou, 12, Universal Images Group/Photofusion, 20; Shutterstock: 1000 Words, 4, ActionPix, 17, Arthimedes, Cover, Design Element, ESB Professional, 11

Contents ▲

Some words are shown in bold, **like this**. You can find out what they mean by looking in the glossary.

What is immigration?

Sometimes it seems as though immigration is always in the news. In simple terms, immigration is people coming to live in a new country. So why is it such a big issue?

Coming and going

Each year, thousands of people come to live in the UK. Thousands of people also leave the UK to live in other countries. But the overall pattern is that more people arrive than leave. Each year the government works out what they call the **"net migration"**. To get this, they take the number of people who arrive in the UK and subtract the number who have left. For the year-long period ending in September 2017, net migration was 244,000. That is more than a quarter of a million people added to the UK **population** in a single year.

Tourists are people who arrive for a short holiday. Immigrants plan to settle and stay.

Many immigrants are children, who arrive in the UK with their families.

Bigger and bigger

Each year, the number of babies born in the UK is bigger than the number of people who die. Add this to net migration, and you have a population that is growing quickly. In 2006, the population of the UK was 60.8 million. In 2017, it was 66 million. In another ten years, it will probably hit 70 million. The United Kingdom is a small country, in terms of area. A growing population means it is necessary to build more houses and roads. It means more pressure on hospitals, schools and local services. But it also leads to a **diverse** population, where people from all over the world can meet and work together.

Who comes to the UK?

Immigration may be in the news, but that doesn't mean that it's a new idea. People have been coming to the British Isles for thousands of years. In fact, you could say that we are a nation of immigrants!

Way back when

Great Britain was actually connected to Europe until about 8,000 years ago. But then rising sea levels cut it off, making it an island. From then on, any immigrants had to arrive by sea. In AD 43, the Romans invaded and took over. They built towns and roads, and spread their laws and language. The Romans had left by AD 410, but their **culture** left a lasting impact.

FAST FACT

The Romans brought many things to Britain, including pet cats, straight roads, heated baths, central heating, firefighters and cabbages!

The Romans built Hadrian's Wall, in the north of England, to protect their northern border.

Anglo-Saxons and Vikings

Shortly after the Romans left, new groups began to arrive. People from Ireland began to settle in the northwest. At the same time, groups called Angles, Saxons and Jutes travelled across the sea from the lands that are now Germany and Denmark. They took over most of England, often fighting with the **native** Britons over the right to the land. But they were determined to stay in their new home. They fought fiercely against the Viking invaders who began to arrive in AD 793.

In 1066, another group, the Normans, invaded from France. They were led by William the Conqueror. The Normans killed the English king and took over the country. All of these invaders have influenced life in Britain. Many of us have ancestors who belonged to one of these groups.

The Normans built the Tower of London after they invaded England.

Slowing down

After the Norman invasion, immigration slowed down. Over the next few centuries, small groups of Jews arrived, followed by people from what is now Belgium. Starting in the 1500s, England's involvement in the **slave trade** led to the arrival of Africans. French **Protestants** began arriving in the late 1500s, fleeing religious **persecution** in their homeland.

In 1948, the *Empire Windrush* ship brought a group of immigrants from the Caribbean, starting a new era of immigration from former colonies.

The British Empire

By the 19th century, the **British Empire** ruled over many other places around the world. These **colonies** were often rich in natural resources, which Britain wanted to control. In the 1800s, immigrants began to arrive from India, one of the largest colonies. People also arrived from colonies such as Australia and Canada.

The overall number of immigrants was small. But when World War II ended in 1945, Britain faced a shortage of workers. In 1948, the British Nationality Act gave any subjects of the British Empire the right to live and work in the UK. After that, large numbers of immigrants began to arrive from current and former colonies such as Jamaica, India and Pakistan.

Immigration today

Immigrants now arrive in the UK from all over the world. **Citizens** of the **European Union** (EU) have the right to live and work in any member country. Hundreds of thousands of them have come to the UK. Many people have also arrived from areas troubled by war, such as Syria, Iraq and Sudan. Others come from the world's poorer countries, hoping for a better life.

Many refugees in Europe are escaping the war in Syria and other troubled countries.

Looking for a better life

Moving to another country is a big decision. Immigrants have many different reasons for wanting to leave their homeland – and just as many reasons for choosing the UK.

Finding a job

Work is the most common reason that immigrants give for coming to the UK. Jobs in the UK often pay better than similar jobs in other countries. Some immigrants are hired by UK companies, who arrange a work **visa** for them. Others look for a job once they arrive. Many immigrants work in factories, restaurants, hotels and on farms. There are also many immigrants working in the health service and in scientific fields.

Many immigrants work in the NHS, providing expert care to patients.

Almost one in five university students in the UK come from other countries.

Student visas

The UK is home to some of the world's top **universities**.
In addition, being able to speak English fluently is a skill that can help workers find jobs, no matter where they live. Because of this, many students come to the UK. They get a visa that covers the time they will spend doing their course. Many of these immigrants will go back home when their studies are completed.

Joining family

Immigration is a way of keeping families together. A British citizen may meet and fall in love with someone from another country. They may be able to bring that person to the UK to get married. Other people leave their home country to join family members who are settled in the UK. For example, a parent might come to live with their grown-up son or daughter.

Fleeing danger

Some immigrants come to the UK because they no longer feel safe in their home country. These people may face persecution because of their religion or ethnic group. They may also be in danger if they speak out about their political opinions. Other people come from countries where war puts **civilians** in danger.

Immigrants are sometimes fleeing a different kind of danger. Their home country may be struck by floods, earthquakes or other natural disasters. There may be a famine, where food shortages mean there is not enough to eat. People fleeing danger often feature in news reports, but in reality, they make up less than 10 per cent of the total immigrants each year.

Many immigrants will brave dangerous journeys to find a safer place to live.

MANAR'S STORY

Manar was 11 years old when she arrived in the UK with her family. She grew up in Syria, where a **civil war** began in 2011. From her home, she could hear gunfire and see warplanes flying overhead. One day, Manar's family decided to leave Syria. They wanted to live somewhere safer.

At first, like many other Syrian refugees, the family lived in an informal **refugee camp** in neighbouring Lebanon. However, many of them ended up living in tents with no running water or electricity. It was not an ideal place to grow up. Manar's sister is disabled, so her family were allowed to come to the UK. They **settled** in Bradford, which is home to other Syrian refugees. Manar is excited about learning English and starting her new life.

Many regions in the Middle East are at war. This picture shows a battle near the Syrian border.

Today's immigrants

Immigration has changed the face of the UK. In 1951, people who had been born in other countries made up only 4.2 per cent of the population. By 2015, they made up 13.4 per cent of the population. In some areas, such as London and the southeast, there are huge numbers of immigrants. In others, such as Northern Ireland and northeast England, there are fewer.

Where do people come from?

Immigrants arrive from every corner of the world. In recent years, many of them have come from Eastern European countries such as Poland and Romania. Large numbers of immigrants also arrive from other European countries such as Italy and Spain. There are still immigrants arriving from former colonies including India, Pakistan and Australia.

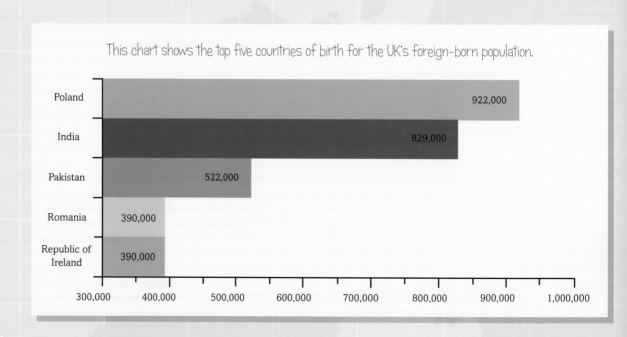

This chart shows the top five countries of birth for the UK's foreign-born population.

Poland	922,000
India	829,000
Pakistan	522,000
Romania	390,000
Republic of Ireland	390,000

300,000   400,000   500,000   600,000   700,000   800,000   900,000   1,000,000

People in the UK have the right to speak out on issues they feel strongly about.

Choosing the UK

Immigrants have many different reasons for choosing the UK. Some come to study or take up a job offer. Others may have family or friends already living here. Thanks to the internet and the popularity of Hollywood films, many people around the world speak English as a second language. For them, it makes sense to choose an English-speaking country.

Other people are attracted by the freedoms and opportunities in the UK. For example, in some countries people face arrest or death if they speak out against the government. But in the UK, people have the right to free speech. The rights of women, disabled people and minority groups are protected by law. The crime rate is low, and health care and education are free and of good quality.

The right to live in the UK

Moving to the UK can be complicated. Many immigrants must apply and be given permission before they come.

Visas

Many people apply for a visa to come to the UK. It gives them permission to live here for a certain number of years, and sometimes to work as well. When a visa has **expired**, the immigrant may be able to extend it. If not, they will have to leave.

There are many different visa categories. Some are for students. Others are for people who have been offered a job by a UK company. There are family visas to allow partners and children of people settled in the UK to join them.

Fiancée visas allow people like Meghan Markle to come to the UK to marry.

THE WINDRUSH SCANDAL

Starting in 1948, many immigrants arrived in the UK from the Caribbean and other former colonies. One of the first ships that brought them was called the Empire Windrush. In 1971, any of these people who were already living in the UK were given the right to stay permanently.

However, the Home Office did not issue any paperwork to confirm this right. In 2017, some members of this "Windrush Generation" were asked to prove that they were here legally. Without the right paperwork they could not do so, and some of them were **deported** unfairly. The government eventually apologised and set up a task force to help these people prove their right to stay.

EU citizens

Citizens of EU countries do not need a visa to live or work in the UK. Once the UK leaves the EU, this may change. The UK and EU are working together to agree the rights of EU citizens to stay in the UK after Brexit.

Prime Minister Theresa May and members of her government were criticised for the way they handled the Windrush situation.

PRIME MI

Refugees and asylum seekers

Refugees are people who are fleeing war or persecution. People who are recognized as refugees have certain protections under the law. To gain this recognition, they make an application for asylum, becoming an **"asylum seeker"**.

The authorities will decide whether returning that person to their home country would lead to persecution. If the application is approved, the person receives refugee status. They gain the right to live and work in the UK for five years. They can access state **benefits**, and may be able to bring family members over.

FAST FACT
A person must already be in the UK to make a claim for asylum.

Many charities offer legal help to people claiming asylum in the UK.

Economic migrants

An **economic migrant** is a person who moves to seek a better life in a different country. But coming from a poor country is not reason enough, on its own, to be given the right to live in the UK. Many economic migrants who arrive in the UK without a visa or a job offer decide to apply for asylum. The authorities may decide that they do not face persecution, and are coming to the UK for economic reasons. If so, their claim is likely to be rejected.

Illegal immigrants

Some people are in the UK illegally. They may have entered on a visa but then stayed after it expired. They may have snuck into the country, for example hidden in the back of a lorry. Illegal immigrants have no paperwork to prove their right to be here. They may have trouble finding work or be denied access to services. If caught, they may be deported.

Immigrants whose asylum applications have been refused may be held in detention centres for some time.

Life as an immigrant

For some immigrants, adjusting to life in the UK may be a challenge. One of the biggest challenges can be learning to speak English. Without knowing the language, it is difficult to speak to neighbours, doctors, employers and landlords. Many schools and charities offer language classes to help adult immigrants. Schools have programmes to help children learn English.

FAST FACT
More than 15 per cent of schoolchildren in the UK do not speak English as their first language.

Language classes are a good way for immigrants to meet people in their new home.

Finding work

An immigrant may not be able to find the same type of job as they had in their home country. They can apply to have their degree or qualification recognized in the UK, but this can take time. If they don't speak English well, they may need to take a course. Many immigrants work in low-skilled jobs, such as factory work or cleaning.

Homesickness

It is common for immigrants to miss their home country, even if they fled because of war or persecution. They may miss friends or family who were left behind, or worry about their safety. Adjusting to the British weather can be a struggle for people who come from warmer places. Even simple things like missing their favourite foods can make immigrants homesick.

Most immigrants receive a warm welcome from their new neighbours. However, some do not. People can sometimes be suspicious of immigrants from different cultures. They may be rude or unfriendly. This may make immigrants feel uncomfortable in their new home.

Celebrating holidays and festivals helps immigrants connect with the local community.

Becoming a citizen

Immigrants often decide to return to their home country. But others choose to stay in the UK, and some of them will eventually become British citizens.

Passing the test

To become a citizen, an immigrant must have lived in the UK for at least five years (or three years, if their **spouse** or civil partner is a British citizen). They must be "of good character" (honest and reliable) and not have broken any immigration laws. They must also prove they can speak English and pass a test on British history, culture and life.

Voting in elections is one of the most important right that citizens of a country have.

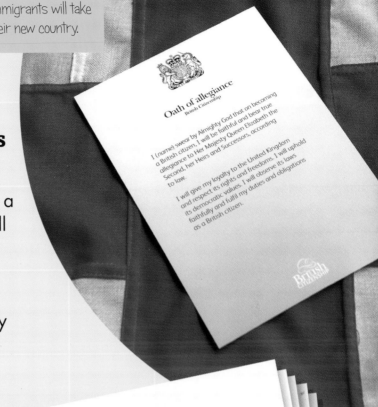

Oath of allegiance
British Citizenship

I (name) swear by Almighty God that on becoming a British citizen, I will be faithful and bear true allegiance to Her Majesty Queen Elizabeth the Second, her Heirs and Successors, according to law.

I will give my loyalty to the United Kingdom and respect its rights and freedoms. I will uphold its democratic values. I will observe its laws faithfully and fulfil my duties and obligations as a British citizen.

Citizenship ceremonies

If an application is successful, the immigrant will take part in a citizenship ceremony. They will promise to respect the rights, freedoms and laws of the UK. As a citizen, that person will now be able to vote and apply for a British **passport.**

MICHAEL'S STORY

Michael is an engineer who was born and grew up in South Africa. His career took him all over the world, but he eventually settled with his family in Scotland. After living there for several years, he decided to apply for British citizenship. He knew that he wanted to stay and raise his family in Britain.

He passed the "Life in the UK" test and proved his knowledge of the English language, then submitted his application. When it was approved, Michael took part in a citizenship ceremony in the Scottish Borders. In front of his family and friends, he took an **oath of allegiance** to his new country.

Leaving the UK

The opposite of immigration is emigration: leaving one country to live in another. Every year, hundreds of thousands of people emigrate from the UK.

Who leaves the UK?

Some leavers are immigrants who were always planning to go back home, such as students who have finished their course. Others might choose to leave because they miss their original home country, or want to be close to family and friends. If they left their original home due to war or natural disaster, the situation might have improved enough to go back.

Many British citizens also leave each year. They move to other countries for some of the same reasons that immigrants come to the UK. These British citizens often move to study, take up a new job, or join a spouse or partner overseas.

Some British citizens move to countries such as Spain or France when they retire, to enjoy the better climate.

KATARINA'S STORY

Since the UK voted in June 2016 to leave the European Union, many EU citizens living in the UK have decided to leave (see page 28). One of them is Katarina, who spent eight years living in London after moving to the UK from Slovakia. She worked, paid taxes and began to feel at home in her new country.

But Katarina found it frustrating that she, like most other EU citizens living in the UK, wasn't allowed to vote in the **referendum**. She felt that after the referendum, the mood in Britain had changed. As an immigrant, she now felt unwelcome.

FAST FACT

In the year up to September 2017, 130,000 EU citizens emigrated from the UK.

I AM NOT A BARGAINING CHIP

EU citizens in the UK are campaigning to have their rights protected after Brexit.

What's the big deal?

Immigration is a controversial topic. Everyone has their own opinions about who should or shouldn't be allowed to come to the UK.

Myth and reality

News reports can be misleading. For example, there is a lot of coverage of refugees and economic migrants coming to Europe from Africa and the Middle East. It would be easy to think that many of these immigrants end up in the UK. However, this is not true. Many more go to other EU countries, such as Germany and Italy. Asylum seekers make up a small percentage of the immigrants arriving in the UK each year.

Newspapers and other media can sometimes give the impression that immigration only brings problems.

NEWS

EUROPE'S MIGRATION CRISIS

Jobs and benefits

Many British citizens worry that immigrants will take jobs from native-born citizens. It is true that most immigrants come to the UK to work. But since 2011, the **unemployment** rate has gone down. This shows that although there are more people in the UK, there are also more jobs for them to fill.

The government provides benefits (financial help) to people in need. Council housing, jobseeker's allowance and payments to carers are all benefits. Some people suspect that immigrants are coming to take advantage of these benefits. It is true that immigrants use public services, such as education and the NHS. But most immigrants from outside the EU cannot claim benefits such as housing benefit or jobseeker's allowance until they have permanent residency, which can take years.

Instead of taking jobs from British workers, many immigrants actually create jobs, by starting businesses.

Immigration and Brexit

Immigration was a key issue for many voters in the 2016 EU referendum. The UK can control the number of immigrants it accepts from countries outside the EU. But as a member of the EU, the UK cannot set limits on immigrants from other EU countries. Many "leave" voters felt that the UK should have more control, and that leaving the EU was the best way to get it.

After the referendum, EU citizens still immigrated to the UK, but the numbers went down. The number of EU citizens leaving the UK increased. However, there are still more EU citizens arriving than leaving.

FAST FACT
In a poll taken one week before the referendum, immigration came top in a list of the most important issues for voters.

The vote in the EU referendum was very close, with a narrow victory for the "leave" campaign.

The Notting Hill Carnival, held in London each year, started in the 1960s to celebrate Caribbean culture.

A diverse nation

Immigration has made the UK a diverse nation. There are people living here from all over the world, and restaurants and shops reflect this diversity. At festivals such as Diwali or Eid, people come together to celebrate different cultures. Many children become friends with classmates from other cultures. They learn to be **tolerant** of different ideas and values.

The future of immigration

The UK remains an attractive place for many immigrants. It is a **democratic** country with high employment, where free speech and the rights of everyone are protected. It is not likely that people will stop coming to the UK. But fears about too much immigration will also continue. Our challenge for the future is to find a balance.

Glossary

asylum seeker person who has fled their home country and made a claim for refugee status in another country

benefits payments made by the government to help people in certain difficult financial situations

British Empire former empire consisting of Great Britain and its colonies around the world

citizen legally recognized subject of a country. Citizens have rights in that country that non-citizens do not.

civilian ordinary person who is not a member of the armed forces or the police

civil war war between citizens of the same country

colony country or area under the control of another country, and often occupied by settlers

culture ideas, customs and social behaviours of a particular group of people

democratic describes a political system in which the population elects representatives to make decisions

deportation expulsion or sending away from a country, usually because a person is there illegally

diverse representing many different cultures

economic migrant person who moves from one country to another to work and improve their standard of life

European Union (EU) group of European countries that work together on political and economic issues

native born in a particular place or country

net migration the number of people who arrive in a country, minus the number of people who leave

oath of allegiance promise to be loyal to a country, person or organization

passport official document that proves a person's identity and citizenship, and allows them to travel to other countries

persecution ill-treatment, especially because of race, religion or political ideas

population number of people who live in a country or region

Protestant member of a Christian church that separated from the Catholic church in the 16th century

referendum vote in which people answer a question rather than choosing a representative

refugee person who has been forced to flee their home to escape war, persecution or natural disaster

refugee camp place where refugees live. Refugee camps are often crowded and have only very basic accommodation.

settle make a permanent home in a place

slave trade historic system in which human beings were bought and sold as slaves

tolerant accepting of other people's differences

unemployment rate number of people in a country who do not have a job

university high-level school in which students study for degrees

visa official permission to enter, leave or stay in a country. Visas are usually stamped or added to passports.

Find out more

Books

Immigration (Our World in Crisis), Claudia Martin (Franklin Watts, 2018)

Immigration (Talking About), Sarah Levete (Booklife, 2017)

Immigration & Tolerance (A Focus On…), Charlie Ogden (Booklife, 2018)

Refugees (World Issues), Harriet Brundle (Weigl, 2018)

Who Are Refugees and Migrants? What Makes People Leave Their Homes? And Other Big Questions, Michael Rosen and Annemarie Young (Wayland, 2016)

Websites

Visit this website to read more about the history of immigration to the UK:
www.ourmigrationstory.org.uk

Learn some of the facts and figures behind the headlines at:
www.bbc.co.uk/news/election-2017-40015269

Read the story of one brave refugee girl's journey to the UK:
www.bbc.co.uk/newsround/36714334

Explore the different types of visas available for people coming to the UK:
www.gov.uk/browse/visas-immigration

Places to visit

Migration Museum at the Workshop
26 Lambeth High Street
London SE1 7AG

Museum of Immigration and Diversity
19 Princelet Street
London E1 6QH

People's History Museum
New Ct St, Spinningfields
Manchester M3 3ER

Index